AMAZING
MINECRAFT
SECRETS
YOU NEVER
KNEW ABOUT

By
Minecraft books

Minecraft Secrets

The Elusive Spider Jockey

One of the rarest mobs in Minecraft, it's a skeleton that rides a spider. Every skeleton has a 1% chance of spawning as one of these.

Fishing For Enderman

It's possible to hook an Enderman with a fishing rod; if you do this while they are neutral they will stay neutral.

Rare Flowers

Roses are more rare than dandelions.

Music Disc

If a skeleton kills a creeper with an arrow the creeper will drop a music disc, which can be played.

Lightening Creeper

If lightening hits a creeper it will become 10 times more powerful, the explosion will be massive.

Saving Glass

Creepers and Skeletons will not see or attack players through glass.

Slowing Cobwebs

Cobwebs will slow down a creepers explosion timer if they are caught in it.

Skeleton Suicide

If you are above or below a skeleton, he will end up shooting himself.

Halloween

On Halloween all the mobs will sometimes wear Jack O Lanterns or pumpkins on their heads.

Helpful Spiders

Cave spiders can poison skeletons, however the skeletons will not die, as he will only have half a heart left.

Zombie Pigmen

If lightening strikes a pig it will turn into a zombie pigmen.

Christmas

Chest will look like gift boxes on Christmas.

Fall Damage

If a spider takes fall damage during a fight it will become docile.

Dangerous Lava

Magma Cubes can't swim in lava.

Hurtful Little Cubes

Tiny Magma Cubes can still hurt the player, unlike tiny slime cubes.

Falling Resistant

Magma Cubes don't take fall
damage.

Pumpkin Protection

Looking at an Enderman with a pumpkin on your head will not turn it hostile.

Only Use When Necessary

Don't place down Obsidian
unless you need to as it attracts
mobs.

Mushroom Island

A rare type of island with a lot of mushrooms and red cows with mushrooms on their bodies, which are called mooshrooms.

Soft Soul Sand

If your boat crashes into soul sand it won't break.

No Trampling

Placing fence under dirt blocks with crops on them will prevent it from being trampled.

Fishing in the Rain

Fishing is much easier in the rain

Invisible Minecart

If a Giant slime gets into a minecart, the cart will become invisible.

Invincible to the Sun

Zombies and skeletons won't catch on fire during the day if they stand on soul sand.

Wool Variety

There are a total of 16 different colors of wool.

Safe in the Mushroom Biome

No hostile mobs will spawn in mushroom biomes.

Breathe Underwater

Bring an empty bucket with you whenever you go underwater, when ever you are getting low on air just use the bucket and a single block of air will appear under water for a split second.

Giant Mushroom

Make any mushroom a giant mushroom by using bone meal on it.

Title Change

Every time you open Minecraft there is a 1 in 10,000 chance that the title will say "Minceraft" instead of Minecraft.

Villager Love

Any villager can fall in love and raise a family. Just make sure that he or she has an empty house with working doors and they will move in a raise a baby villager.

Neutralizing Cactus

If a spider takes damage from a cactus it will become neutral.

Avoid Endermen

Looking at an Enderman through transparent blocks will not make the enderman go hostile.

Friendly Spider

If you throw a chicken egg at a docile spider and hit it, the spider will stay docile.

Saddle Up

If you can find a saddle, you can put it on a pig and ride it, but you can't control it.

Minecart Driving

If you put a saddled up pig into a mine cart you can drive it like a car off the tracks.

Easy Fuel

Use any wood block to fuel the furnace, anything from stairs to signs.

Charcoal

Smelt wood logs to make charcoal, which can be used to make torches.

Renew The Tools

Craft two low durability items together to combine their durability.

Torches Everywhere

You can place torches on furnaces and crafting tables by placing glass behind them and trying to place the torch on the glass!

Torch Blocks

You can place blocks on the sides of torches; you don't need to place extra blocks to do the same thing anymore!

Torch Weight

Torches can hold any amount of weight in sand or gravel on top of them.

Minecart Lava

With a wall of lava between you and your mine cart it's possible to right click it and get it, going through the lava, without getting hurt!

Quick Switch

Looking at any block type and clicking the center button the mouse will automatically switch to that block if it's on your hot bar.

Location, Location, Location

Hit F3 to open the debug menu to see your coordinates of where you are.

Quick Craft

Shift-click the output of the crafting table to instantly move it to your inventory!

Sapling Fuel

Saplings can be used to fuel the cooking of one block in the furnace.

Creeper Proof

Any structure built out of Obsidian will survive a creeper blast.

Squid Spawn

Squids will spawn not just in oceans but waterfalls and lakes as well.

Cobblestone maker

When lava and water touch cobblestone is created.

Obsidian

When water touches a source lava Obsidian is created!

Stop the Water

Ladders, signs, and trapdoors stop water in their tracks! Use it to keep water from flowing where you don't want it.

Fire Proof Wood

Wooden slabs are practically fire proof. They won't burn nearly as easily as regular wood.

Hidden Wires

Red stone wire can travel right through any type of half slab blocks. This lets you hide your wiring easily!

Pressured Water and Lava

Lava and water can be held, without spilling, by surrounding a source block with 4 pressure plates.

Break Your Boats and Minecarts

Use a bow and arrow to quickly and easily destroy and dispose of your boats and minecarts.

Lava Furnace

Lava buckets will power a furnace for 1000 straight seconds. Use it as a tool to easily keep your furnaces going.

Melon Destruction

A diamond sword will break melons faster than any tool.

Pumpkin Breaking

A diamond axe will break pumpkins faster than any other tool.

Quick Mushroom Soups

Milk a "mooshroom" with a bowl to quickly make a mushroom soup.

Break Cobwebs

Use either shears or a sword to quickly break down any cobweb.

Ice Sand

Placing an ice block underneath soul sand will make it much much slower to walk over.

Golem Falls

Both iron and snow golems are immune to fall damage.

Glowstone Glass

Glowstone breaks just like glass so be careful not to hit any after you place it.

Quick Add

To add an item straight to your inventory from a chest just press shift and click on the item you want.

Slow Down the Jumping

Jumping too much will quickly empty your hunger bar.

Only Sprint in Emergencies

Just like jumping sprinting will empty you hunger bar even faster.

Cook Your Meal First

Light any chickens, cows, or pigs on fire before killing them, as the meat they drop will already be cooked.

Conserve Your Fuel

Only use coal to smelt/cook when you need to smelt/cook at least 8 items. Use wood for everything else to save on fuel.

Destroy Gravel/Sand

Place a torch underneath any large amount of sand or gravel to quickly and automatically destroy it all.

Don't Burn

Always carry a potion of fire resistance while mining, that way you can use it and save yourself if you ever fall in lava.

Pack a Lunch

Never forget to bring food with you wherever you go, your hunger bar will always go down eventually.

Bring the Essentials

No matter what you are doing or where you are going, be sure to always pack all of your essential tools.

Safety Water

Keep a safety bucket of water with you where ever you go in case you fall into lava.

Mark Your Trail

Whenever you go out exploring
be sure to mark the way you
came, it's far too easy to get lost.

Block Incoming Attacks

Block any attack you can, it will half the damage you take, it will even allow you to survive a creeper explosion.

Armor Up

Armor will let you more easily survive any fight.

Enchant Everything

Make sure your weapons are enchanted; it will help with a huge variety of things from mining to fighting.

Leave a Survivor

If you kill all the animals in a group they won't respawn for a very long time, just leave a single survivor and they will respawn much quicker.

Fast Farming

Use bone meal on crops to quickly grow them to full size.

Go Peaceful

If you just want to play survival mode for a while without dying just turn on peaceful mode.

Be Fire Safe

Don't play around with fire, it's a stupid way to die and lose your items.

Make a Step

Leave the bottom log of a tree you're cutting down so you can use it as a step and reach the very top most logs.

Keep the Best

Avoid using anything but the best tools as the game goes on, everything will be faster and better.

Stay Away

Never kill a creeper with anything other than a bow, or else you risk the chance of your dying.

Set Your Own Spawn

Sleep in a bed anywhere to reset
your spawn to that point.

Create a "Checkpoint"

If you are far away from your spawn point and don't want to lose your progress, just reset your spawn to nearby.

Dig Smart

Never dig straight down, you'll trap yourself and make it hard to get back out.

Cave Mining

Once you find a cave fully explore it and mine anything of value, it's quick and easy.

Keep It Lit Up

Mobs will only spawn in the dark, so keep your house lit up to avoid them spawning nearby.

Use the Best

Don't waste your time mining always use your best pickaxe.

Lava Buckets

Never keep lava buckets in your hand; the chances are you'll use it by accident and die.

Easy Meal

Spider eyes will fill you to more than 90% hunger but they will hurt you in the progress.

Gold Tools

Never use gold for any sort of tool, the durability is terrible and it takes a while to mine anything.

Leave it to the Big Tools

Only mine valuable resources with a good pickaxe or else you risk destroying the block.

Perfect Timing

It takes 10 minutes and 40 seconds for you to smelt any 64 stack of something in a furnace.

Sneak and Reach

If you sneak or crouch you won't be able to reach as far.

Safely Dispose

Use cactus instead of lava to destroy unwanted items, its safer and more efficient.

Double Durability

Using a tool for something besides it's purpose will make it lose its durability twice as fast.

Easy Does It

Hold down shift while walking and building on any cliff faces or ledges so you don't fall off accidentally.

Bonus Section

Thank you for reading this book. I hope you enjoyed it. Gaming is very near and dear to my heart and I enjoy every moment I spend playing my favourite games.

If you liked this book, and are interested in more, I invite you to join my "Customer Only" newsletter at http://awesomeguides.net/. I publish all my best stuff there for free, only for my customers.

If you're a Minecraft fan like I am, I'm sure you'll like my other best-selling releases:

1. <u>Minecraft: Awesome Building Ideas for You</u>
2. <u>Amazing Minecraft Secrets You Never Knew About</u>
3. <u>Minecraft All-In-One Quick Guide! Master your Minecraft skills in Everything!</u>
4. <u>The Amazing Tale of Steve: A Minecraft Novel</u>

5. Minecraft: Amazing House Designs with step-by-step instruction
6. Awesome Minecraft Traps To Defend Your Home
7. 50 Awesome Minecraft Seeds That You NEED to Know
8. Amazing Minecraft Maps You Will Definitely Enjoy!
9. Minecraft Amazing Redstone Contraptions
10. The Ultimate Minecraft Guide to Tekkit: Discover the Advanced Mods for Minecraft!

In my strategy guides, I share neat tips and tricks to help you get better at gaming. From Candy Crush to Dragonvale, you'll find strategy guides for a wide variety of addictive games.

1. The Last of Us: Amazing Strategies and Secrets
2. Dragonvale: The Complete Guide: Amazing Cheats, Gems, Breeding and MORE!

3. <u>Candy Crush Saga Best Tips, Tricks and Cheats!</u>

We also have an awesome Minecraft course on Udemy – an instructor led online learning platform.

1. <u>All about Minecraft: A complete educational course</u>

Have fun gaming!
Egor

Made in the USA
Lexington, KY
13 May 2014